"WHAT THE FREAK DID I HIT?"

A True Story of Tragedy and Tenacity

by

Tommy Fergerson
and
Kisi Thompson

WANDERING BARD PRESS
http://wanderingbardpress.com/

ISBN: **0615719805**

What the Freak Did I Hit?

Tommy Fergerson

Kisi Thompson

DEDICATION

I want to dedicate this book to my wife Sandy for all her time and understanding; to my children for accepting the changes in our lives; to Skip Moreau for having confidence in me to continue skydiving; and to David for opening the doors to make my amputation financially and emotionally possible. Special thanks to the many people who have given their love and support to help speed my healing, who have encouraged me to get back to living, and all those who will be putting up with me for many years to come.

BLUE SKIES!

FLIGHT 343

April 30, 2011 was a normal jump day. As a jumpmaster, I had gone up and jumped with two sets of students in the morning. This afternoon's jump was my three hundred and forty third of my career and was a "fun jump" for the instructors or experienced skydivers. These fun jumps are often what we call an "up jump", a skydive from a higher altitude with plenty of time to play during freefall, and time to navigate or fly our canopies to the drop zone and hit the center target of the landing pit. A bull's-eye is great, but landing in the footprints of the jumper before you is a feat that earns cheers and bragging rights.

Skip was our pilot and took us up to the "top", about 9,000 feet of altitude. Rick and a gentleman from

Mexico were going up with me, and I was going to film them. Being an instructor, I typically wear a helmet camera to record my students, to capture the memory, help them see their form, and learn to improve on their next jump. As the plane gains altitude, we shout through any last details, check that the camera is on, and cheer each other on with high-fives. Once we got to the top, the pilot gave us the thumbs-up signal; I opened the door and stepped out onto the strut and framework of the wing. I worked out to the end of the wing, so I could look back at the door and film the other two exiting the plane and releasing into their falls. They both had clean exits, so I then released and fell backwards, watching the plane fly away with its whirring engine. When the altimeter on my wrist read 7,000 feet, I flattened out with my belly to the earth, got stable, arched my head back and pulled the ripcord at about 4,000 feet. The canopy deployed normally and was fully stable by 3,500 feet. Winds were coming out of the south, blowing me away from the drop zone towards the airport hangars. I watched the windsocks and did a couple turns to try to work back to the east and get closer to the drop zone. All of a sudden there was a huge gust of wind at my back pushing me south, gaining speed and starting to force me downward. I did not think I could get to the landing zone, even though the windsock on the ground was now pointing from the west. What I was feeling pushing me around and what the socks were indicating were two different things. The ground was coming up fast and my only thought was that I was going to hit the trailer. I didn't want to try a last second hook turn for fear the speed and angle would spin me right into the trailer and stab me in the back. The more I looked at the trailer and tried to steer away from it, the closer it got. Then everything went black. My trusty helmet camera filmed the whole incident. It has been reviewed by experts, including some former Golden Knights Skydivers, and has had hundreds of thousands of hits on the Internet. Though my memory has gaps in it from the time of impact until getting to the hospital, the camera kept recording every moment and every word. It feels odd to return to the accident repeatedly, and watch myself, to think about what could have happened, and still not remember being there.

The guys on the ground hesitated after the impact, thinking that I was dead. Once they heard the gurgles and moans, they rushed over to help. Dillen slowly undid the strap and took off my helmet to help me breath a little easier. Unknowingly, the camera still rolled and captured the whole story from the outside. My first memory was Neil checking on my shoulder and trying to keep me from getting up. He was sure there was a broken collarbone and probably broken arm, the way it was just flopping next to me. The pain was not that bad yet, but my possible concussion or shock was keeping me from thinking and feeling accurately.

"What the freak did I hit?!?" I asked.

"The trailer" was the response in unison.

I was speaking and trying to move around. I felt like I had to get up, get back to the hangar, and get back home. The guys called Skip and told him what had happened, and he raced to my location. They asked me how I felt, what my name was, where I was, and what was hurting. As soon as Skip got to me, he asked me the same questions.

"What the freak did I hit?!?" I asked.

"The trailer," he responded. The guys told him that was about the tenth time that I had asked that same question. Skip knew I had to get from the rural Fremont County airport to the hospital quickly, so the guys eased me into the pickup and we got on the highway. I could tell that Skip was getting frustrated with me because I kept asking him what I had hit. That is when he started to think that there was more damage than any of us could have imagined.

Skip ran into the hospital and grabbed a wheelchair to take me inside. My right arm and right foot were fine, but the left side of my body was weak and beginning to hurt. The hospital did preliminary X-rays, CAT scans, and MRI. Neil had followed us to the hospital, and took pictures of my cut face and left shoulder that was quickly turning bright red. We talked while waiting between tests, trying to fgure out what had happened from everyone's different view of the accident. After their preliminary review in Canon City, they suggested that we go to a larger hospital in Pueblo. Skip and I were ready to jump back into the truck and make the fifty minute trip. The director of nursing came down and spoke to us, explaining that she did not think it was very wise to make the trip on our own. Being in an ambulance would be safer and would be better prepared if my condition worsened. As I am a small business owner between insurance companies at that moment, my fnancial thoughts were overriding my medical thoughts. I could not afford the ambulance trip and I didn't feel that bad. Skip was a volunteer EMT, so I figured he could handle a broken collarbone. After some arguing back and forth, she convinced us that the ambulance would be the best transportation. They got me ready for transport with a neck brace and their standard safety procedures. Skip and Neil jumped into their vehicles and headed back to the hangar and drop zone. They put me in the ambulance and we headed for the Pueblo hospital.

Now keep in mind, that I still had not yet contacted my wife, because there was no definite news to give her. My wallet, keys, and phone were all still with my street clothes and gear in my locker at the hangar. The EMT in the ambulance said I could use his phone, so I asked him to dial my home phone since I could not see the numbers without my glasses or through the bloody bandage from

6

the cut above my left eye. I gave him our home phone number and he dialed so I could talk to Sandy. I told her we were on the way to the Pueblo hospital and that I would see her there in a little while. We both worked in the medical profession, so our conversation seemed very clinical, until we had more information about my condition.

When we got into the emergency room in Pueblo, the doctors started doing tests and asking the same questions that everyone had been asking me all afternoon. Things started becoming blurry and floated into a slow blah, blah, blah. I woke up a day or two later, not knowing what was happening except that I was in more pain that I had ever felt in my life. At first, I thought it was just the drugs, but I had three arms. My right arm was fine, absolutely no feeling in the arm that I could see and grab with my right hand, and excruciating pain in an invisible arm that wrapped around me. I could not tell where the pain was, where it originated or how to make it stop. All I knew was that nobody is supposed to have three arms, and this amount of pain cannot be endured for very long.

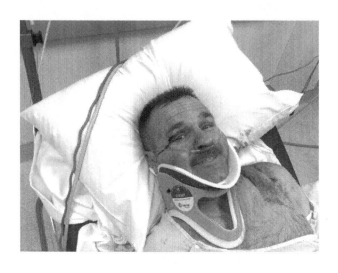

The day of the accident in the emergency room.

WAKING UP – THE WEEK OF WONDERING

I woke up on the third day with Sandy at my side. The pain was unbearable except when I was drugged out and sleeping. The morphine was auto dispensed through an IV, but the button had to be pushed every ten minutes to release the medicine. If I fell asleep for thirty minutes, the pain would be at such a high level when I woke up, it would then take three or four ten minute intervals until the pain would finally come back down to a level where it only felt like my fingers were being smashed with a giant hammer. I did not know what the test results had revealed or understand how much damage had been done to my body. In an ironic sense, the damages that were most visible, would be the most minor, and would heal up quickly. In those first days I went through multiple procedures. They used four stitches to close the cut above the right eye. This was opposite the side of impact, so my helmet or goggles must have cut my forehead. I had a bruised lung, which made the hospital breathing exercises extremely difficult. I broke bones on my left side that included the scapula, collarbone, coracoid process, wrist, ribs, and three broken bones in my left foot, the last of which they repaired with surgery then immobilized in a monster padded boot. My damage on the left side also included a dislocated shoulder. The worst injury was to the brachial plexis, which controls the sensory and motor skills of the shoulder, arm and hand. My probable concussion was almost overlooked because I was coherent and trying to take control of my situation from the seconds right after impact. The one indicator that things were jumbled in my brain was that I did not understand or remember what had happened in those few moments after the accident. Only after viewing the film and listening to others, would we later piece together all that had happened. The "coracoid process" and the "brachial plexus" were the hardest words to understand. Little did I know at the time, they would have the most impact for the rest of my life. The brachial plexus had avulsion, which means the nerves that control my left arm were ripped out at their "roots" from my spinal column, stopping all communication from my arm to my brain; ceasing all motor and sensory skills. I owned a perfectly strong and healthy muscular arm, with no control or feelings.

Neil, the instructor, had taken photos of my injuries at the Canon City hospital and brought them when he visited me at the Pueblo hospital. We laughed at how awesome the video was from my helmet camera. Many friends from skydiving, from the hangar, customers from my business, and others I knew from parental activities with my kids came to visit me. When I was conscious enough to hold a conversation, we talked about the accident, how I was now, and what I planned to do. My main concern was getting back to work, keeping the business going, taking care of my family again, and then getting back to skydiving. Matt, one of the tandem jump instructors, came and sat with me one day for three to four hours. Most of our conversation was small talk, but then he offered to take me back up in the air on a tandem jump. He just knew that I wanted to return to the sky, to fly again, and he wanted to help make that possible when I was ready.

The pain in my foot was annoying, the dried blood around my head stitches was cracked and crusty, the bruised lung and dislocated shoulder made any horizontal position feel like resting on a pile of rocks, but the pain in my left arm was the most intense that I had ever felt. Up until this, I had thought the time I got body slammed off the edge of the wrestling mat in high school was the worst. Hitting that bare concrete floor with my lower back and hips sent shock waves all the way into the back of my head. The match was not over, so I shook it off and went back to wrestling. I remember that next morning as a kid, I could not get out of bed, and there was no feeling in my legs. Good thing for the Army crawl. I pulled my pajama pants to guide my legs off the bed, slid across the linoleum floors, got into the kitchen, ate a bowl of cereal, but could barely reach up from the floor to put the dishes in the sink, then went back to bed to read, and rest up. By Monday morning, I was able to get up and put on pants and shoes, but still could not bend over to tie the laces. Moving around and walking to school, loosened up my muscles and by noon, it felt a little sore, but mostly ok. Many years later, during a physical for a job at the Gooch Packing plant, the doctor was concerned that my back had been broken and had calcified itself to heal. It seemed fine from my side, so he agreed the mend was adequate. In comparison, that pain was bearable, because I could feel what made it worse and could avoid doing that particular thing. The pain coming from my arm did not match the chunk of flesh that just hung there. The sensations of pain in my arm were sharp, hot, crushing, twisting, but my eyes stared at that quiet appendage and everything looked fine from the outside. I just wanted to get away from it, to stop it, to figure out how to slow the attacks of pain, and to calm the waves of sensations. Right now, the ten minutes of morphine were keeping me together, but morphine cannot go with me to work.

Later on, maybe that evening or even into the next day, a very calm gal came to visit me. She was a mental health evaluator who wanted to find out if I was handling my situation properly. It was explained to me that I had

13

been in a horrible accident and they were there to help me. That made sense, but her voice seemed very passive and textbook, as if she knew something in my chart that nobody wanted to tell me. We talked about the last few days and all the medical data, and then she asked what I was going to do. Well, I was going to get out of the hospital in a couple days, go home, and get cleaned up, go to work, and then go skydiving. Her pen quit moving and she spoke without looking up. She wondered if I truly understood my injuries, and that I may not get back the use of my left arm. I thought a minute, and that made sense, so I continued to explain my situation. I am a small business owner, so if I don't work, I don't get paid. I have a family with eight kids, and I am the father. Skydiving is my passion, loving the wide variety of people that I get to meet and continually testing my skills and abilities. She scribbled a few more notes, closed her notebook, and graciously said our time was completed. It seemed odd that the hospital would do a psych evaluation. I'm ok, just busted up a little bit.

Sandy, my wife, and Adorea my daughter, found a wheelchair so that I could get up, get cleaned up with a mini-bath, and get out of that boxy room. It felt so good to go up and down the hallways, to see out, to see the bright blue skies and watch the chopper come and go. The nurses were starting to get frustrated with me. When they came to get me for tests, I would be cruising around with the wheelchair. Friends started to look for me in the halls before coming up to the room. My friends Petie, Matt, and Sandra came and visited one afternoon. It was encouraging to hear their laughter and feel their energy. There was absolutely no progress on my left arm, even after more MRIs and CAT scans. Having no "good news" often led to odd conversations about what may become reality. We got to laughing about the many grim possibilities, like a low budget "B" movie when it is so ridiculous it is more silly than rude. Another thought that if they amputated the arm, then we could have it done like taxidermy and used as a business card holder for my office. Amidst our howls and laughter, the last thought was that it would be handy to have it stuffed, to take with me in the car, just in case I needed a hand. The jokes continued to roll, saying the worst words with gallons of gusto and smiles. True friends can help with the darkest situations. They jokingly confirmed what my gut and subconscious had been saying for the last few days. It is a blessing to have friends that can be horribly honest, because their words are spoken out of love and with respect.

Multiple neurologists came through, read the tests, flipped through the charts, and often left silently without even touching me. I was starting to feel invisible, that they did not think I could understand my predicament, or the possibilities to fix it. In between tests and specialists, I was to get training and rehabilitation so that I could go home. With the multiple injuries, the rehabilitation became a comedy act. A gate belt that was supposed to wrap around my middle to help the therapist hold me up to walk, could not cinch around my broken rib. Crutches under my left arm were worthless, since my left hand could not hold or grip the handle. A cane in my right hand would only tip me over towards the oversized gauze on my left foot and trip me. Pushing a wheel chair with only my right hand made me do circles in the hall. At this point, about the only physical therapy I could do was hopping on my right foot and trying to keep my ribs from banging together. To me, there was nothing else the hospital could do for me, so I might as well go home and go back to work.

The doctor at the hospital was concerned with how I could manage at home, and was not ready to release me. Sandy and I both have medical backgrounds, so we discussed our possibilities and options. We did not think more time at the hospital could help me heal any faster than being at home. We thought we were going to have to be discharged with an AMA (Against Medical Advice) form, but the paperwork finally came together and we were able to leave the hospital. It felt so good to be home and feel like my life was coming back together. I missed the noise and chaos of the kids and all the activities.

Back to work in my office.

BACK TO WORK

Getting back to work was one of my priorities. Earning a paycheck was important but, more than that, was getting back to my customers and solving their problems. Serving a variety of people and businesses keeps the days challenging and exciting. I never know what will walk through the door and what it will take to make them happy. My right hand man, Mark, had been working like a maniac while I was in the hospital. Mark had hired his brother, Matthew, to help fill in while I was gone. My daughter, Stacy, was filling in as she could between her school and her own medical needs. My shop is in a split-level medical arts building, with my area in the garden level, which is four steps up to the entrance from the parking lot and down eight more steps to my front door. On Monday morning I got up bright and shiny and went to work. Mark came out and got the wheelchair into the office. I would have to hop around until my foot got out of the walking boot, or until my arm could help support me with crutches. The first day was not very productive, mostly getting acclimated to the physical limitations and awkwardness of not being able to just "do something." The pain medication was helping my foot, but the pains in my phantom arm grew exponentially throughout the day, until I was ready to collapse later in the afternoon. I was on 600 mg of Neurontin for the phantom arm pain, and Percocet for the physical pains of my broken ribs and foot. I did not like the vagueness and drugged feeling from taking pain medication; I needed to have all my wits about me and a clear thinking mind in order to do my job well. On the first day back to work I only made it until two in the afternoon. We set up a cot in the back storage area so I could lie down and get little catnaps throughout the day. When I was working at the hospital on split shifts, going to school full time, and running the shop, that same cot had given me wonderful hours of sleep throughout a hectic and changing schedule. Now, the waves of exhaustion would suddenly crash over my thoughts like an arctic storm over a breakwater. I would argue with my muscles and eyes, but would only find that I had lost the argument, when I would awake to find my forehead having the imprints of my keyboard, watchband or whatever was on my desk. These moments of utter emptiness and total loss of energy made me think back to when I was working in the nursing home. Back then, I could not understand how people could just sit and do nothing. Looking back, I'm glad I took the extra time and empathy with my elderly patients, to encourage them to keep trying.

Most people that came into the shop did not know what had happened to me. Most of them saw the sling and assumed I had shoulder surgery, rotator cup repair, or a broken arm. Since there was no ambulance dispatched to the accident, there was no news, no police report, no newspaper article, no blog or blurb, just word of mouth between friends. Many of my customers asked what was wrong and had great concern. Others asked only because it felt more awkward if they did not say something.

Outside the shop, people now look at me differently, if they look at me at all. Most will glance over and return a weak smile, or they will avoid eye contact and pretend that they did not even see me. I know how clumsy I am with a left boot, left sling, right stitched brow, and hunched over broken ribs. After my second day back at work, the wheelchair was doing no good so the wheelchair was set in the back. I just had to get around the best I could. It reminded me of one of the multiple times when I was on crutches as a kid. The largest cast was from my buttocks all the way to the tip of my foot. It all started in the barn on a hot summer day. If you chased the chickens, caught one, held them by their rough yellow feet, and tossed them straight up in the barn, they would squawk and flap around, and then land on the high rafter beams. The chickens were not so smart, because they would fly down to the ground and we would get to do it all over again. As I was running around chasing them, I stepped into a mason jar and cut the tendons above my ankle. I screamed to my sister "I'm going to need stitches – get mom!" I ran to the trashcans where I fell down from exhaustion. My mom was on the phone and thought my sister was just joking and playing a trick. All of a sudden, I heard mom holler, "Get up here to the garage and get in the car right now!" I knew it was bad, because mama didn't even make me go in the house to get cleaned up before getting into the car. She still had groceries in the car and did not bother to take them into the house first. She drove us to Hell Center Medical where they were able to stop the bleeding and clean up my foot, but they were way too small, and did not even have an operating room. Mom and I got back in the car and headed to the big hospital. My stomach was queasy from the heat, the ride, my foot hurting and we did not even have lunch that day. Mama said I could have a banana out of the bag in back, if that would settle me down some. At the big hospital, the doctor tested my toes and took me right into surgery to sew up the tendons in my ankle. While I was on the operating table, that banana came back up and started to choke me. Luckily, the doctor could see why I had aspirated the banana; my tonsils were so swollen and infected, that I could hardly breathe. We did not see that choking as a blessing at that time, but our local doctor was giving me penicillin shots in my leg twice a month to fight joint pains and rheumatic fever. A couple weeks later, when they took out my infected tonsils, all the joint pains and fevers were cured instantly. The surgery on my foot and tendons lasted almost eight hours, and then I was sent to a recovery room. The room was big, white, very noisy, and smelled like mothballs. I could hear all the nurses talking outside and their squeaky shoes coming up the hallway. They finally put me into a room with another kid. He was in a body cast from his waist down, because a house fell on him. We talked and became friends right away. He had some of those little green army men, so he would throw me some from his bed so we could play. We got tired of that game, then started playing 'Attack War' and we would throw the army men at each other to see who was the best shot and the best blocker. After so many shots, all the toys would be on the floor, and the kid in the body cast could not get up, so I would hop around and get them all, divide them in half, and the war would start again. After several days, the doctors were disappointed that the tendons were not healing properly, so they took me back to another eight hours of surgery and sewed them together again. The doctors could never figure out how just moving around in bed or wiggling a leg could have torn those tendons loose. I never told them about our game, but they made sure the stitches would stay together underneath a cast stretching from my buttocks to the tips of my toes. That cast was so hot and itched like fire ants crawling through it. The doctors did come back and cut a trap door on the top of my foot so they could check the sutures and healing of the incisions. They sent me home soon since the tendons were now mending. I got really good on those crutches – walked to school, did chores, played king of the ditch and even did some things better. I could take real big steps when running, and had fantastic launches when doing the long jump. I gained another three feet on my jumps, except the sand would work up into the cast and rub like crazy.

I was not as limber this time on crutches, almost forty years later, but I got so I could balance on the crutch and one foot in a boot. Eventually I only needed the crutch for balance and depended upon my good leg for strength. The last stage was kind of hopping around on my strong leg and using the booted foot as a counter balance, like someone with just a stump of a leg, swinging and rocking for stability.

At work, it was hard to remember that what my brain told my hand to do, would not really happen. That arm just hung there in the sling. I would push the screwdriver and turn with my right hand, but my left hand would not hold the other side and the computer would slide all over the bench. What had been almost fifty years of habits, just didn't work anymore. Customers would hesitate to help, but would grab at the last second before I would push a computer off the backside of the counter. I had to mentally think about the simplest things that I was doing. I strengthened quickly and could work for about three hours and nap, then start again. Being on business sites, at stores, or at customers' homes was the most challenging because I never knew what new obstacles may be in the way or what new technique I would have to use. I am becoming much more limber as I am forced to use my knees, feet, teeth, and my right arm to do double duty. Nothing is quick and easy, everything has to be thought out first, sometimes two or three times.

While I was at one customer's home, my arm kept

falling out of the sling as I crawled around working on his computer. David was bothered by my limp arm. He could understand and realize what a frustrating time I was having. At that point, we did not know what the progression would be; we had another four to six weeks before the EMG. Even though getting back to work was helping me physically and mentally, I still needed a way to pay all the doctor bills. The accident happened while changing between insurances, and became a big fiasco. I finally did what some had suggested, went down to CICP at St Mary Corwin, and asked for help. They did set up payments in accordance to what I made, based on supporting the four kids still at home. That gave me so much relief, so I was not feeling so guilty about having medical debt. Other items were still not covered and we had to pay out of pocket, but we did have some breathing room.

Daily items became the things that frustrated me the most. How do you button shirts? How do you zip your pants? How do you put on deodorant? How do you do these things? How do you tie your shoes? Sandy would tie my shoes, but I felt really stupid asking. This was

27

something I could do when I was four years old. I tried buying Velcro shoes, but they were all clumsy, heavy and not very comfortable. With the pins and damage to my left foot, my left shoe sizing is half to a full size larger than my right. I just could not justify buying a pair of shoes for each foot. I special ordered orthopedic fancy super shoes, and they were still big and clumsy. My legs needed the comfort of good athletic shoes, so I had to learn to tie shoelaces with one hand. The challenge was on. After checking out the internet and watching YouTube videos, I made fine adjustments to fit my needs and now I am very proud to say that I tie my own shoes. What is a five-second process for most people, now takes me five minutes, but I still can do it by myself. My little grandchildren and I both get excited and dance around when we finally get our shoes on.

Solo jump with stump still wrapped to my body with gauze and duct tape.

WHAT'S ON YOUR MIND?

Because of all the video captured with my helmet camera, my skydiving prior to the accident, the accident itself and jumps during my recovery are all available to be viewed in real time. YouTube, Facebook, and my website put my skydiving, the accident, the healing, my friends, and family on display for the world to see. My words and stories are all from my perspective and from what I feel in my heart. The details and technical side of my skydiving are documented with film and videos. The best part is that everyone worldwide has an open forum, to share, criticize, or strive to help others. Sometimes the greatest encouragement comes when I least expect it, and other comments surprise me. I chose to leave the postings and comments open, so that all perspectives can be seen. The only comments I removed are those that are vulgar or directed specifically to a member of my family. Read for yourself some of the hundreds of comments left on my website or in response to my YouTube videos. To maintain accuracy and fairness, all comments are in their entirety exactly as posted, only the user names have been removed.

"It is so nice to see that you are not beaten by the accident and that you can get back to what you love to do. Great inspiration."

" You are cool man I will attempt one handed flare on my next jump, respect."

"lol they jacked his helmet cam"

"OUCH!!"

"Good reason why I will not try this at home"

"Dude, so sorry for your loss, but at least you did not lose the use your legs or life. Sounds like you suffered a concussion and your buddies should have picked up on that by the time you asked what you had hit for the 3rd time. They also should have immobilized you and call that ambulance. Anyway, glad your OK, even if a little altered from how you

began."

"Damn i can see the importance of landing against the wind, not make any turns at low altitude and flair at groundlevel now. Glad your alive, sorry for your arm. My teacher told me – Do not focus at the point you do not want to land at, because you will for sure land where your focus is at. This thinking strucks me every time i see a bad landingspot which im close, and I have succeeded sofar ⌄"

"Glad to see you still jumping mate."

"Hahahahaha"

"blue skies"

"I hope this isn't insensitive, but you handled that situation like a boss. I don't know many people who can mangle their bodies and react by saying "Aw crap, that sucks." I hope you were equally as "boss" coping with the loss of your arm....god knows I not as badass as you. Good luck to you!"

"This is one of the reasons I will never skydive. Thank you for sharing though."

" I saw your website a few days ago- glad you got back on your feet and enjoying doing what you love. From some of the negative comments I've seen looks like there's a lot of envy, i.e. people who don't

understand the courage you had to keep goind and doing what you love to do. My hats off to you!"

"You are such an Idiot..."

"Don't call a ambulance call a cop there faster! And you don't have to pay for the ride!"

"Its called target fixation, what you look at is where you will go"

"its ok to swear"

"just by how you filmed this makes it the coolest sky diving vid ive ever seen"

"his cussin language is soo funny⌄"

"IM SORRY BUT YOU LOOK UNEXPERIENCE SKYDIVING"

"Thanks for the entertainment!!!!"

"Did the guy claim for damage to the trailer? ;-) You made the same sound as me when I had my skydive accident. Urgh, arrgh, ophf. I got carted away on a golf trolly....with a shattered spine! But being British I was apologizing to everyone instead of cursing. Arch, Look, Reach.....for the 1st aid kit!"

"Dumbass"

"im a morotcycliste n we call that target fixation"

"I am so sorry that happened to you. I could see the winds blowing hard. You made the right choice. Had you turned I think you would be dead. I would have done the same thing as you. Sorry for your injuries. God Bless. Stay strong."

"It's the risk of not living that drives s to jump… not the risk of death. I made my first jump as a 2nd date suggestion. She suggested it & booked it for us and I wanted to look macho because I like her. The truth is, the thought scared the bejesus out of me. I HATE heights.   The girl is gone now to another state, but that 2nd date suggestion changed my life. Great frieds, great fun, & a bond that is beyond words. You should try it some time… you might just like the feeling of living."

"Well any retard who jumps from and plane and risks there life deserve this"

"im surprised you weren't swearing…:O"

"Ouch, I cringed quite a lot watching this. Good to know you survived this. I hope your skydiving in the future is more successful."

"jeez mister, I have to hand it to you you've gotta a lot of sand sir. that was a horrible accident, you totally kept your composure, even managed to edit your expletives, hope you healed quickly, bro"

"Best wishes. Thank you for sharing this tragic event with others and hope it provides some discussions about safety at DZs everywhere. Do you still plan to fly someday?"

"What's up with some of these rude comments? You did something they are uncomfortable doing, so they say "you got what you deserved!" On person says " I hope you learned your lesson" Are these people insane!? You lost your ARM! Have these people NEVER done anything even mildly dangerous. What if one of these narcissists went to a pool and decided to jump off the diving board, but they slipped, and broke their neck. How would they feel if you said to them "you're an idiot for trying that!?"

"What does one expect when they jump out of a plane. This is why I will never be sky diving. You are lucky to survive. I do hope you learned your lesson though."

"Why would you jump from a perfectly good airplane?"

"isn't it hard to type with 1 arm?"

"Thank God you're alive"

"Glad you're alive. Object fixation happens to the best of us sometimes."

"man I hope you are doing OK. It must have

been tough to post this video. I thank you. Its really valuable for other jumpers. This sure looks like a classic case of "Target Fixation". If so, it happens to the best of us. There is one tree at our DZ and it's crazy how many people hit it. Blue Skies...."

"Wow, dude, that sucks. If I were you, I'd disable the comments on this video so you don't have to endure all the jackass commentators. Every skydiver makes mistakes; it's just unfortunate that you weren't able to recover from your's and escape without injury"

"seriously, YOU HAD 10000 FEET to avoid the ONLY OBSTACLE in 1 square mile and you nailed it. TEN THOUSAND FEET!!!!!"

"awesome dude!"

"Great man!! I have a brachial plexus injury and you make my day!"

"I think you made me lose my fear of flying"

I decided to leave the posts and comments open, so the hope and encouragement can be shared and enjoyed by others. The negative and hateful words can be discouraging, yet their anonymity takes away the personal sting, and they are just words of people who were not in my situation. Some comments push me to try harder and never give up. In the beginning, it was difficult to ignore some comments, and just accept them as comments or opinions. Some of the mean and vulgar posts crept into our family life and started tensions and heated debates between us. Seeing my kids have to explain or defend was hard to watch, but made me proud that they would stand together. In the end, the people who see the long-term goals are very encouraging and supportive. I think back and wonder if I truly could have done anything differently, maybe been five minutes earlier, had a flat tire on the way to the airport, gone rafting instead, or slept in that day, but I cannot change that now. I am here in the present, with only two choices; give up or keep moving forward. I want to continue, to beat the odds, to encourage others, to pass on my mistakes so others don't have to repeat them, to find options in the medical realm, and to really enjoy the second chance that I've been given. I am amazed at what I can do with this limited body, the new places in life I am going and the wonderful people I now see, because of my accident.

MONEY DOESN'T GROW ON TREES

It had been about three months since the accident, and work and home were getting back to a routine of work, kids' school events, home life and skydiving. My clumsiness and phantom pains were the most difficult to blend into life. I received a standard call from one of my customers, David, who called and was having computer troubles. After a little diagnosis over the phone, I thought it was the power supply, so packed one up and headed to his house. I had not seen David for almost a year, so he was giving my arm the questioning look, but never said anything. He watched me work and was surprised with what I could do with only one hand, and the other in a sling. While I was crawling around under the desk working, that dead arm kept falling out of the sling. I would reach for another screw for the power supply and the arm would fall out of the sling again. Finally, David could not stand it anymore and spoke up saying, "Man, I can't stand to watch you work like that, we gotta do something. You have a family to feed; you have all this to do, and you're still working. I don't think I would still be skydiving after something like this, but that's your choice. We gotta do something, that arm is terrible." This blurted information was good to hear from a friend, he spoke his heart honestly and out of concern. I thought it was weird that he questioned the skydiving, as he is a retired Navy Seal. He had jumped HALO jumps (High Altitude Low Opening) which means they get out of the plane at an extremely high altitude of 20,000 feet (often times with oxygen) and open their parachutes at 800 feet from the ground. I was amazed that he would be concerned, since he had made many jumps. David asked how this had happened. Because I had multiple field visits that day I told him the condensed version and encouraged him to check out my videos on YouTube.

My situation was really bothering David, because he is

a caring type person. David was 67 at that time, and took care of his parents full time, who are both in their late eighties. He feeds them, does the laundry, gets them up, cooks for them, cleans for them, gets them to bed, and has his own life. This guy is amazing in all that he does, and now he is looking at me as if he should do something for me. I am thinking my life is not that big a deal in comparison to what he has going on; his life is much harder than mine is. As I was finishing up, David said, "Tommy, we gotta do something about that arm." I explained that I may need to have it amputated, but we were still waiting on EMG tests and specialist diagnoses. David commented on how I could get so much accomplished. He felt that I could do more with one arm than he could with his whole body. He wanted me to show him how I buttoned my shirt, and then took me in to his mom and dad so I could demonstrate for them also. It felt funny to show off something so simple, yet it filled my heart that he had a true appreciation, since he dressed and undressed three people everyday. Taking the time to practice and learn a different way to do something with one hand takes time, but the independence is worth the effort. By the time I was leaving, David was adamant that something had to be done with that arm. As I reached the door, David said, "That thing is a hindrance, what if something happens to it? It needs to be cut off. It's a hindrance, it's in the way, you gotta feed your family, you gotta take care of everybody and get back to work, you can't have that thing like that." I was honored that David had so much compassion for me; he is just a really great guy. He said he would watch the live accident videos and other videos of my pre and post injury jumps. He and his old Navy Seal buddies all watched, and each had their own ideas about why it happened.

About three days later, David came lumbering down the steps into my shop, with a stiffened Frankenstein walk, swaying from side to side, getting his large six foot plus body through the door. David can barely walk, because he was hurt in Viet Nam, injured as a police officer and paralyzed in a car wreck. He was paralyzed from the neck down, staying for over two and a half years in a hospital bed. He understands being trapped in your body and mind, locked in that prison with the phantom pain. He understands what it feels like when your brain creates sensations and pains to compensate for the nerves that are not sending back signals from the flesh of a paralyzed body. His most vivid example was the weight and distress from a bed sheet. He explained how a fresh cool sheet sliding across his chest had once felt so refreshing, but was now white-hot sharp nails tearing out every hair follicle as that weight brushed against his skin. During paralysis, the brain takes over and reassigns pain and sensations to each of these hair follicles, because the muscles cannot give a response that the brain is seeking. It sounds crazy and is difficult to understand the phantom pain, so my connection with David was such a relief; I am not insane. When paralyzed, David felt like thousands of nails were being driven into him, just from the weight of a sheet. He laid there stark naked because the pain was so unbearable. He would look at you, just being able to move his eyes as people would walk by his room, totally naked and very trapped. He would wrinkle his face when I told him that any pressure across my cheek would send electrifying pains down my third and imaginary arm.

David rambled into my office and said, "We got to get you fixed. I can't stand watching you; we got to do something. You tell me how much it's going to cost. We got to get you fixed and get you going."

I replied, "Who are you to talk about what needs to get fixed and what we need to do. You have your parents to take care of and all your responsibilities."

David countered my protest with, "They are old, have lived a good life, and are pretty well set up for the rest of their life, whereas you are young, you have a family to feed, you have to take care of them, walking around with that arm that's useless. You gotta feed your family and take care of all those kids. I got an idea where we could raise all this money. It would be great if you had a solid figure of how much the amputation will cost, but I can understand how difficult it would be to get an exact amount."

I told him that from the research I had done from the internet and other people that I had spoken to that had had amputations, it should cost between twenty-five thousand dollars and eighty thousand dollars.

David said, "Tommy, you need not be so prideful, I want to do this. Will you let me help you??"

I was still in the dilemma of self-insurance and

between companies of what they would carry and what was pre-existing. I had contacted the Denver University Hospital that helps people with extreme cases. My doctors had sent in all the forms that I needed to have this arm amputated, but the hospital responded that they would not do it because I was not critical. Hospital policy does not allow them to give a specific reason why they would not do it; they just send the rejection notification.

David had contacted his neurologist, who had retired to Washington, and explained the whole situation. This neurologist thought we would have gotten better results with the application if we had not focused on the phantom pain, but on the things that you can physically see, hold, or grasp. We needed to resubmit the application focused on the atrophy, "bed sores" from the sling, risk of infection, possible bone breakage, and the hazards of keeping the arm attached. David said that if the new application was denied, then he wanted to go to different TV stations, radio programs and newspapers, up in Denver and Colorado Springs to raise money. He thought we could raise about twenty thousand dollars.

For the remaining sixty-thousand dollars, he offered to give me the rest out of his own pocket, with no payback. David stood there with that gentle sway, "I need to know if you will let me do this."

This was one of the few times in my life I was speechless, and did not know what else to say except, "Like, wow, geez, uhh, thank you ... yes." It was so emotional, that I did not know what to say nor do, I could not get my head around why he wanted to help me.

"Then let's get the ball rolling. I've spoken to a lawyer already to set up the paperwork so you don't have to pay this back, and there are different things needed to be done through the government so you don't get taxed on this as income and lose 25 percent of it," said David in a business like fashion. He had printed up about 40 pages to fill out to get this set up as a non-taxable donation. All would have to be filled out before starting any fund raising, or it would count as income and would be taxable. Actually, I was overwhelmed and shocked. David still does not realize how big in the mix he was, to get everything started and to have so much influence on so many people.

During the paperwork process, more connections and

networking came together.   When David was at his doctor's, he thought he recognized my daughter Adorea. It turns out that David's doctor worked with the doctor with whom my daughter worked.   David and Adorea talked about the accident, the upcoming fund-raisers, and me. Adorea was not aware of all that they were trying to accomplish, but she wanted to see what she could do to help too.   She got on the internet, on Facebook, and started sending messages out to raise money for my amputation.

All this stuff was happening daily, but the everyday work and home life were happening also. Knowing David and Adorea were working things from the backside while I was applying on the front side to insurance companies, to doctors, to Colorado Indigent Care, made the rejections a little easier to take. I finally got a neurologist from Denver to review my files and be painfully honest about my prognosis. He said there just was nothing there, but an EMG (Electromyography) would be the final test.

During a visit to my pain specialist we spoke about the phantom pain and why the morphine, Percocet, and

Oxycontin were not helping. The pain was in my brain, literally in my mind, not in the flesh and muscles. He said an EMG would prove if the physical pathways still existed. Instead of making a trip to Denver to get an EMG, he could do one here locally. Several customers and people that had been through an EMG warned me about how much pain I was going to be in, and that it was the worst pain because the test literally sends electricity through your nerves. After those talks I got the test scheduled and was all psyched up to go through this painful test.

My pain specialist had a fellow doctor with him on the day of the test, who was learning how to do the procedure. I really enjoyed that, because I could listen in on all the technical aspects and learn the details. He placed the spring hoop electrodes around the bases of my fingers, stuck needles into the various muscles, and sent an electrical frequency to test for a pathway. As he went from muscle to muscle, he was explaining to her what each one did and how it functioned. The test results are seen on a screen that looks like a green military sonar detector, and is audible through sounds like radio static.

When he started the test, a calm buzzing noise intensified up to a loud noisy garbled static like multiple radio stations.

"Do you hear that? That is not good. There should not be any sound, and you should be jumping off that table as the electrical signals bolt through the nerves from one end to the other. There are no connections to your nerves; you are literally doing nothing," he said in a very matter of fact way. He had worked with my phantom pain for months, and knew the massive amounts of medications and frustrations that I had. I liked his no-nonsense approach to fixing things. Throughout the testing, he was explaining to the intern how these nerves should be firing, from where the needles are inserted into the muscle, down to the sensors around the fingers. When nothing is working, the nerves are destroyed. He explained that this arm was useless and probably would never come back, so we needed to get rid of it. The very first thing that popped into my mind was, "Can I keep it??"

The doctor just looked at me, and then thought I should be able to keep it, since it was my arm. He then focused on me in that very patient, very understanding manner and asked me why I would want it. I explained that a friend suggested that I could taxidermy it and keep it on the counter at the shop as a business card holder, or like the people at the drop zone, they wanted me to mount it in the flying bird position. The intern could not hold back the smile and laughter any longer. She was primarily an obstetrician, and explained to me that when she delivered a Jewish baby, the parents may request that they save the placenta. Their faith believes that what you come into the world with is what you should take when you exit this life. She did not know how they saved it and really did not want to find out, but because this is a religious aspect, she must respect it as their physician. I needed to become Jewish before the amputation! My doctor slowly shook his head in disbelief, but smiled slightly, knowing that I was accepting my grim condition with humor and laughter. I think I had already come to grips with my condition when I was in the hospital right after the accident. Having three arms, my good right one, my dead left one, and the invisible one, could only mean that one would be leaving me.

After learning the EMG test results, Adorea spoke with her office and explained my situation, and that I needed this amputation. Her doctor spoke with a vascular surgeon, and again explained my situation. The surgeon and his anesthesiologist were in the same network, which the insurance would cover, so that piece of the puzzle was solved. The surgeon thought the amputation would be between five and six thousand dollars, and would let me pay it off over time. Adorea called and told me all the good news, but said I needed to meet with the surgeon for a consultation. I figured it would be weeks before an appointment. She said come in today, but it would be $100 for the first interview. I knew I could scrounge up the money before the appointment, and was excited to finally get some real answers. Sandy, Adorea, and I went to his office and discussed the details of the amputation. My surgeon is very meticulous, quiet and serious, and probably even more so with the gravity of an amputation. He looked at my arm and spoke about the three types of amputations: upper, lower, or mid amputation. A mid-amputation would be best for me, to get rid of as much dead weight as possible, and have less physical area for future complications. He described the procedure, the recovery, and possible complications of the amputation. When he was done, there was a lull in the conversation as he looked at my file one last time. I asked, "Can I keep it, the arm? I'm Jewish!" My wife and daughter looked at me, looked at him, looked at each other, and then burst out in laughter. If Adorea was still a teenager she would have given that blank look, said 'Da-aad', and rolled her eyes, but she has known me way too long to be surprised. He methodically looked up from the file with large clear eyes and simply said, "No, it's mine." On a more serious note, I explained that the surgery needed to be done on a weekend, so I could be back to work on Monday. He said we could do the surgery whenever, but I would need at least three to four days in the hospital to recuperate.

The appointment was on a Friday and I contacted David on Saturday, to tell him what all had happened. David had planned to leave that Monday, going to Denver to contact newspaper, radio and TV stations for the fundraisers. He said that he was sad and happy: happy that he did not have to leave his folks alone, yet sad for the fact that he did not feel like he had helped enough, that he was not a part of my healing. What he did not realize is that he got the connections together and rolling. He wanted me to keep in contact to hear how things were going in case something came up or did not work out. It bothered me that he was sad, but it was so phenomenal that he had done so much, because he cared. My daughter had already received money from a few places, so I told her to quit, that people had to stop sending money. She knew who had sent in money already: Dionisio $500, a cousin sent $100, and the drop zone raised $350 from people just dropping money into a jar. The surgery was estimated at $5,000, and the office manager said that the doctor would only charge $2,200, making it cost ten payments of $220 a month, which was workable. I had all this donated money, so I went back to Jennifer at Dionisio and said that I did not need this money now, that things have worked out miraculously well. She is a contract customer that I work for regularly. She said that she would not take the money back and to apply it on whatever medical bills we had.

"Tommy, you don't realize, you're my one-armed skydiver, we got to take care of each other," she told me.

It is hard to accept help, especially when everyone else is scraping to keep their own businesses running. People almost seemed embarrassed or did not know what to do because of my pride. It was so hard for me to accept. I felt I needed to do it by myself, but people really want to be a part of it. The same as when David said, "Tommy, you got to swallow your pride and let me help you. That's just what people do." The cousin that donated the money would not take it back either, and during this time, he had shot his finger off. He is a gunsmith by trade, and that is what he does for a profession. He was cleaning a pistol, thought he had emptied the chamber, and accidentally shot his finger off. He could not believe it, he is 52 years old, and has cleaned thousands of guns; it was a crazy accident. Surgeons tried reattaching the finger two times, but were not getting good results. I told him I am getting my arm taken off since it is not working either. With all this happening at the same time he lamented, "Man, the Fergerson's are losing body parts like crazy." Another cousin chimed in and said, "I'm losing my mind...does that count too?" It sure is great when family sticks together through all times.

Because the amputation went so smoothly and so cleanly, the amputation surgery was only $962, and guess how much had been raised? That's right, $950, so we were able to pay him off right after surgery. It was amazing how much the surgeon did without charging, and how many people stepped in to help. It all started from crawling under a man's desk and flopping around like a fish, that God put everyone in the right path. The mental stress of struggling with that arm flopping around frustrated me, but literally carrying around a fifteen pound weight swinging alongside me, was physically exhausting too. The arm was withering away quickly, and within a few months from when the amputation was performed, I was starting to get back to my new normal. An odd thing I have seen since the amputation is that people see me and say, "I'm sorry", but I'm not, because it has opened so many doors and I have met so many wonderful people.

One day a customer that needed her laptop worked on, came into my shop, saw my condition, and wanted to hear my story. We had been in a business-networking group ten years before and ran into each other occasionally since then, usually when her computer was dead. A few weeks later, I was helping a customer take all their equipment to their car when she drove up with a big black trash bag. I figured it was a bag full of used cables or spare parts, since she is an electrician and likes mechanical stuff. We chatted about work, family and my progress as we walked from the parking lot back into the office. She hesitated a second and then said, "Tommy, I have something for you, but I don't want to offend you or hurt your feelings." I could not image what could hurt my feelings. She reached into the big bag and pulled out a blue flannel coat. "Try it on; I wasn't sure of your size." That seemed really weird since Sandy and I had just been shopping for a winter coat. My coat from last year has a zipper, and now I cannot hold both sides to align a zipper with only one hand. I stuck my right arm into the sleeve, raised it straight over my head and did a rumba dance like move to get the left side of the coat to swing around my left shoulder. I reached for the buttons, but the jacket had already come together. She had sewn magnets inside the material between the buttons so it would line up and close, so the buttons were in the proper place and I could fasten them with one hand. "Look in the pocket," she urged me. There was one fleece glove, with a metal "D" ring sewn to the cuff. "Put it on the hook by the right pocket, now push your hand into it," she instructed. I slipped the ring on the hook, the glove dangled in place, and then I slid my hand into it. This was the first time I did not have to use my teeth, my knees, a countertop or my foot to put on a glove. It was awkwardly silent as I held back the tears, until she finally said, "Well, what do you think? The left sleeve is sewed into the pocket so you don't get it caught in doors, if it's too baggy, I can alter the sizing, if you don't like it, we can modify it however you want, it's just material. I hope you like blue. It was the only one I could find without a zipper." All I could do with my eyes tearing up, was give her the biggest hug. She took action. She thought about my difficulties and came up with solutions. So many people have stepped up and helped, just because they can.

Tommy in Texas, 1972.

FULL CIRCLE

The doctor appointments, money, insurance and test results all were falling into place for the amputation of my left arm. Logically, my mind and heart knew the amputation was the right thing to do, but there was an odd sadness creeping around the edges. I was almost fifty years old, and was kind of attached to my arm. In looking backwards, I guess all the events in our lives add up to make us ready for the next hurdle we face. Some decisions have no questions or doubts; they are automatic with no wavering.

My childhood home in Abernathy Texas was full of adventures, playing King of the Ditch, catching rabbits in irrigation pipes, jumping off the roof, hiding in the hayloft, riding bikes, and driving tractors. The best times were those spent at school, especially playing football or participating in any sport. I rode the bus to school as often as I could, to save gas money for my car, so I would have enough gas to drive to work. I was not necessarily a bad kid, but I was full of energy and spoke my mind. I liked getting people to laugh and enjoy themselves.

It seemed like I had a special place in the hearts of most of the faculty, even though I spent many hours in the principal's office. Miss Gough was my Language Arts teacher and she loved to teach about Shakespeare. She would hold that book and walk around the classroom reading to us, explaining what all those old words and phrases meant. She would lecture us about the importance of character, and that how people saw our spirit could affect our whole life. She would always say, "Good grades and good citizenship, you cannot have one without the other, unless you're Tommy!" She was usually extremely serious, except when I would take her coat from the rack and wear it. I could hear her voice all the way down the hall, "Tommy Fergerson, you come back right now with that coat, it's cold outside!" I would bring it right back, as everyone in the hallway had a good laugh, including Miss Gough.

Every class had special opportunities. In science class, we would take a mouthful of butane from a cigarette lighter and light it, like a flamethrower. The best part was impressing the girls, and the hardest part was not being caught. I did it a couple times, and then a fellow student tried. Just as he was ready to ignite his breath, the kids all hollered that the teacher was coming. He instinctively tucked his face downward to hide his mischief. Of course, the flames burnt upward and caught his hair on fire. In the midst of all my screaming, I patted him out and luckily, he was not hurt, except for his hairdo. Because our class was so large, we had two teachers, Miss Martin and Miss Robins. They both took me to the office where Miss Martin demanded that I receive punishment. I think Miss Newton loved me; she defended me. She explained that I did get the fire put out so he was not hurt. She said it was quick thinking and that the screaming came from everyone in the classroom, not just Tommy. Principal LeMoin patiently listened to both sides. He gave me three licks with a paddle and then Miss Martin made me sit in front of the class. Not just in the front row, but at her desk, for the remainder of the semester. On that big desk that we had to share, Miss Martin always had a large ivy plant. That plant seemed to die about every other week and she would bring in another plant. She dutifully watered and cared for her ivy, but it would always wilt and die. Miss Martin never did figure out why her ivy plants always wilted, not knowing of the castor oil that I kept feeding it.

One day in Mrs. Beasley's class, she was reading a newspaper article about dinosaurs, and then asked if the class had any questions. My hand shot right up into the air and I blurted out, "Did you ride one when you were a kid?" She turned around quickly, with her hands on her hips and that short red hair swinging around her face. "Well, yes I did, and he had a tiny brain, just like yours Tommy" she said calmly as she walked to the door. "Outside! Now!" She pointed to the hallway. I gathered my books, knowing I was headed to the principal's office. The class all giggled as I left the room and she followed right behind me. "Now follow me, Mr. Fergerson," she said as we walked away from the offices and towards the auditorium. She opened the large auditorium doors and said, "Sit down; I want you to watch something!" I could not imagine what was going to come next. She walked down the center aisle and started a slide show of her trip to Paris with her husband. She asked many questions throughout the pictures, if I liked the places, if I would ever travel, what I wanted to be, and where I wanted to go in life. I mostly nodded and agreed that it was very beautiful. She sent me back to the classroom, while she picked up the projector. As soon as I got into the classroom, everyone asked how many licks I got and if it hurt a lot. I told them that I just watched a slide show about her vacation, and then they all called me a liar. Mrs. Beasley came into the classroom with the projector and picked up her attendance book. The class all begged to know if it was true that I saw the slide show, or if I got licks. She confirmed that we had watched the slide show. The whole class burst out with "Why? That's not fair!" She squared off with the classroom and boldly stated, "He's my pet." The silence was deafening, and everyone's jaw dropped. That was the weirdest punishment I had ever received.

Coach Aldridge and Principal LeMoine called me into

the office and questioned who was throwing snowballs at a basketball game. They asked who did it and I told them that it was me. They were surprised that I was honest about it; and then questioned me as to who brought them into the gym. I would not tell, because that was being a snitch. Another time, Mr. LeMoine was waiting for me when I got off the bus coming to school. We went to his office, because a window in the door by the bus stop was broken. He questioned if I knew anything about it. I knew about it, because I had broken it while leaning on the door waiting for the bus. Since I worked, I usually had some money on me, so I handed him $20 to cover the cost of the window. He did not punish me, because I was honest and covered the repairs. He always watched me, yet he spoke to me like a man instead of a kid.

Miss Bryant's class was my favorite, probably because I usually slept through it. My eyes would get so heavy, that I just could not hold them up anymore. I would promise myself, that I would just close them just for a few seconds. All of a sudden the class would be laughing, as I jerked awake with a loud pig snort. Miss Bryant would sweetly ask if I had a good nap, and continue class as if nothing happened.

My daily schedule was very routine – got up, did chores, rode the bus to school, rode the bus home, did chores, went to work, and started all over again. Many of my teachers and friends would see me working at the Dairy Queen until they closed at midnight or 2 A.M. When my driver's education teacher would see me at work, he would smile and ask how my car was running, knowing that I was underage and only driving with a permit. It was a small town and everyone knew my family and what happened at home, even the sheriff. I kept busy at work and school. The days that I did not work I would sleep, from the time my chores were done until the next morning. School was my only reason to get up. Some days I would be so tired from working the night before, I would miss the bus, and have to drive to school if I had enough gas. The ugly day finally came when my mom was forced to choose between me, and her new husband. I almost shot him in the head for beating her, and she still chose him instead of me. I drove to school that day with all my stuff, to clean out my locker. I waited until everyone was in class, before I went inside.

Miss Bryant's room was directly across the hall from my locker. She watched me for a moment through her window, and realized that I was not just late, but leaving. She came across the hallway, kneeled down beside me, put her hand on my back, and asked, "What are you doing Tommy?"

"We're moving," I told her a partial truth.

"No you're not, your family is staying here, only you are moving. Why are you quitting school?" she asked with no judgment, but with a million more questions behind those eyes. "Tommy, please, promise me, that whatever happens, you'll get your high school diploma, please."

I nodded my head, but could not look at her. I did not want to leave school, it was the only place I liked, but I had to find a place to live and get a job. I went to the office to check out and say I was moving away. Principal LeMoine pulled me into his office for the last time. He knew how good my grades were, and how much I loved sports. He offered to let me stay with his family in their spare room, promised that I could play football for two more years, and that I could stay in school and graduate.

I appreciated all that he offered, but I just couldn't; it just wasn't right. I had to take care of myself.

I did roofing work, odd jobs, and whatever I could without an education. I bounced around working as a welder and was moved up to a shipping/receiving clerk. I even talked to an Air Force recruiter, but since I was underage, and did not have a diploma or GED, they would not accept me. GED classes were held about forty miles away from Lubbock, in Petersburg, Texas, but that did not seem important at the time. The military gave an ASVAB test every couple of weeks to see what people can do, to find out what would be a good job for them. It was something to do, so I gave it a shot. I was very amazed with the results; it showed I was off the charts in electronics, even though I really wanted to be a cop or military police. My ASVAB scores got me into the Air Force, so now it was my time to serve during the Iran Contra Affair. Boot camp went by quickly. The physical part was routine. I had always been in sports in school and since I did not have a vehicle at boot camp or tech school, I ran everywhere. I was one of the few guys that actually gained weight at boot camp; it was great to eat as much as you wanted three times a day, everyday. The mental part was easy, because I was not afraid to die. I wanted to be part of doing something bigger than myself, I wanted to be part of something important. My drill sergeant took advantage of that drive, and pushed us all to do everything like it was our last day on earth. I was fearless, because I had nothing to lose. Marksmanship was easy, since I had been hunting since before we went to grade school, and my dad was extremely strict. If we did not kill, we did not eat, that is just the way it was.

My Lieutenant volunteered me for a competitive shooting and endurance team. My team traveled all over competing against the different military branches and then in the international arena. We did well in competitions, but the British would always beat us. I was so frustrated when we kept losing to the British; I had to learn how to beat them. There was a slight language barrier from British to Texan, but I spoke with their team captain and asked how they trained. When we got back to base, I got permission and we started training and putting together another competition team. My idea was to over-train, to make the British training schedule look like grade school gym class. I was able to compile a team of boxers and marathon runners. Having exceptional athletes on the team meant that I was now the weakest member of the group. Instead of training four hours a day, we trained eight to ten hours a day six days a week, in full gear with flack jacket, packs and boots. The competition included thirty obstacles, including a zip line, fifty-foot tower, sixty-foot drop, a watercourse, and combat course in the first two miles and then another six miles of running. We were determined to beat everyone, but especially the British. The next competition would be at Pope Air Force Base. Our team was the best team we could assemble, but now I was the slowest member on the team. In years before, Sgt. Jesse Garza and I had actually carried other teammates backpack style along parts of the course, so that we could finish. At this event, our team crossed the finish line together. We had to wait for all the teams to run the course, before they would announce any of the finishing times. As they started from the bottom up, we were discouraged when we did not hear our names. In second place were the Brits, and with a time two full minutes faster than second place was, our team –

Dyess Air Force Base.

While in the service, I fell in love, got married and had two beautiful children. My life was starting to feel like a dream, like things were coming together, but that vision was short lived. For whatever reasons, my first wife turned to alcohol, drugs and other men. My heart was broken, but I did not have time to grieve, because I had to fight for custody of my children, Farley and Adorea. In 1985, men seldom won full custody, no matter the condition of the mother. My fight seemed even harder, because I still loved my wife but I could not accept the results of her reckless actions. I promised my children that I would fight to the end of the world for them. After hiring one of the fiercest lawyers in Texas, I got custody of the kids, and could calm down and start living again. This worked well until the kids were in their early teens and my ex-wife wanted them for Christmas Break. Being teenagers, my kids decided they wanted to live with their mother. When she did not want to bring them back to Colorado, I went to Texas to pick them up. With the difference of jurisdictions my custody decree meant nothing to the police in Lubbock, Texas. They instructed

70

me to hire a lawyer and go back to court. After months and piles of money, I went before the Grand Jury to plead my case for the return of my children. The jury could not believe that a single dad had gotten custody of the kids originally. When all was said and done, the kids came home with me to Colorado. In the eyes of the judge, it was in the best interest of the children to return to Colorado with me.

Healing up after the amputation.

LOSING AN OLD FRIEND

It feels like my whole life has been training for this amputation decision. The hard times when I wanted to give up, when I would lie in bed and shout up to God, "Why me?" was now coming together. The last week before the amputation, millions of thoughts started going through my head. Many people have been so supportive, yet I've had others blog or email me that they think I'm totally irresponsible for participating in a dangerous sport while I have children in the home; that I'm a glory hog, a wanna be paratrooper, a dangerous threat because I encourage others to chase their crazy dreams, and a greedy sensationalist. These words can sting, and bring moments of doubt, that maybe I do deserve this, that this is my punishment for all the mistakes in my life. I can only wallow in these shadows and doubts for a short time, or I would fall into a life of negativity and self-pity. I saw a quote on a Facebook page that seemed very wise, "Your negative words can only hurt me, if I choose to value your opinion." When I was a kid, it was even simpler, "Sticks and stones may break your bones, but words will never hurt me!" I find being comfortable and true in my own heart, keeps balance for the people, words and attitudes that come into my life.

We planned the amputation for a Friday, so I would have a couple days over the weekend to get over the anesthesia, before going back to work on Monday. The day before the surgery, it seemed like years of emotions were flooding through my heart. As I was getting my bag ready for the hospital, I sat on the edge of the bed staring at my arm. I started to get teary eyed, thinking of what had been and knowing by tomorrow it would be gone. This arm that had held my babies, the arm where my wife Lola died after shooting herself, the snuggle spot while eating popcorn on movie night, the arm that made up half of my superman dive, and a lifelong companion that was going to be leaving me. The surgery went well without complications. My surgeon did a wonderful job keeping his word, and my arm. The gauze and wrapping on my stump made it look huge, but the heavy unbalancing weight was gone. I felt like I was going to float away. The anesthesia and exhaustion took me a couple days to get over, so I relaxed at home and enjoyed the time with my family. Monday morning came too quickly, but it was going to be an adventure working with my new body.

The physical side of the amputation went relatively smoothly. The wound healed nicely and there was no infection. The stump is only about three inches from my armpit, so stays mostly out of my way, but there is no muscle control at all in it. After all the bandaging came off, I found it more comfortable. Crawling under desks and leaning over computers is when it would flop forward or backwards. Anyone watching me would usually cringe, since it looked like it was all dislocated, but I cannot feel anything except the motion of the weight and the individual hair follicles. Over time, my right side has strengthened and fine-tuned, in opposite proportion to the left side shrinking and withering away. I have been very fortunate with all my bones, cuts, bruises and surgeries healing quickly.

The mental side of my injuries, however, has been a constant battle. My emotional shock, grief, and acceptance of my physical status happened immediately, and was more of a technical sequencing of events. Dealing with the phantom pain has become a full time job. I've spent hours researching, talking with others, asking doctors, trying different medications, looking into neuro-therapy, and it all comes back to one thing – it's literally all in my head. Now my efforts are to retrain and refocus my brain, so it can understand that my arm no longer exists. The power and determination of the mind is extraordinary when it processes the phenomena of phantom pain.

PHANTOM EVIL

The room was totally dark and quiet, except for the occasional truck running up the highway. I lay there against the cool sheets, thinking about my schedule for tomorrow. Most of my customers knew about losing my arm, yet some struggle between their curiosity and their upbringing that taught them "it's not polite to stare" or to "just be nice to the poor man". These were the few quiet moments that filled my soul; that gave me the strength to get up again tomorrow. I find it's easier to talk to God in the dark, maybe because that's when the rest of the world is quiet and I can hear His voice most clearly, when I myself am still. These moments of slumber and peace anchor my course for the day, ready to battle whatever surprises my brain had for me today. As I floated in and

77

out of one of those colorful, cartoon dreams, I could feel something hot and sticky holding my fingers together. It was burning hot and strong, shrinking, tightening harder as I fought against it. I leaped out of bed to turn on the light and make sure my wife was not burned also, but I could not reach the light switch. I could not straighten my arm, my hand was tight as a baseball, the glue was melting my skin, and my eyes could not understand what I was feeling, for nothing was there. The needle stabs of the hardening glue raced up the highway of invisible nerves to the center of my brain, screaming for me to wash it off and to stop this burning, melting attack. Everything was in slow motion, I could hear my heart beat speeding faster, my lungs sounded like those of an angry bear, and my eyes squinted to make sense of what they couldn't see. I raced to the shower to wash it off. I took off my t-shirt and that pink stump just hung there, with little white crosses where the stitches had recently come out. It just hung there, limp and lifeless; no glue, no flames, no skin melting, nothing, except the red, sweaty, contorted face in the mirror staring back at me. I thrashed through the top drawer by the sink, searching for the Neurontin, taking another 600 mg, adding to the 3000 mg already taken today. I fought that white childproof lid that any kid could open in a millisecond. The water would not come out fast enough as I slurped right from the faucet, because I could not hold the pills and the cup at the same time. As I slowly stood up straight, that stupid left eye was winking back at me. The left side of my face tightens up in direct relationship to the pain in my arm that was amputated last month. The heat and strength of the glue eased a tiny bit as my thoughts were now focused on the left corners of my eye and mouth, which were now being slowly pulled together by an invisible metal thread. As I tried to flatten the bulging muscles in my left cheek with my right hand, the skin and muscles of my left forearm started peeling off of the bone, as if a lumbering giant was calmly pulling off a hangnail, then smoothing it back and pulling it off again. The chemicals in the pain blockers eased the severe contraction of my left hand, the sticky glue started to evaporate, and the squint of my left eye relaxed a little, but I now had skin and flesh hanging from my left forearm. My mind raced as I stared in the mirror. My eyes see a 48-year-old man, with a well-healed mid-arm amputation, in decent medical condition, and a silly looking farmer's tan line on one arm. I will have to get out in the yard without a shirt and tan up this chicken white belly before I go on vacation. I would not want someone gawking at my winter tan lines. The laughter burst out of my lungs, and the broad smile shot a tearing lightning bolt through my left forearm, yet I was standing there laughing. I felt flushed and embarrassed, like a 13-year-old boy flexing his muscles in front of the mirror, examining a body that was changing before his eyes. Just then, an ivory sleepy face peeked around the bathroom doorframe.

"Dad, what are you doing? Are you ok?" asked my teenaged daughter.

"Couldn't sleep, this extra arm is keeping me up." I answered.

"Need anything?" she asked, and I shook my head.

"Kay, g 'night" she whispered as she continued down the hallway to her room. The tears welled up in my eyes then fell to the hard tile floor, scattering around my feet. That little girl suffers from rheumatoid arthritis and lupus;

her young thin legs swell up and her knees grind so much that she can hardly walk by 3:00 in the afternoon. She must have heard me up, because she was awake too.

My body stood there, exhausted and clammy, as if it belonged to someone else. What I feel and what I see are so completely different that I sometimes wonder if I am going insane. My doctors say that upper body amputations are so much more intense because the arm has about a million nerves in it, compared to a leg that only has about ten-thousand nerves. My nerves are separated from my spine, pulled back like a broken rubber band, physically in place, yet not connected at both ends. Being a computer guy, the doctors explained the nervous system to me in this way. The brain sends signals or pings out through the nerves to billions of points throughout the body every nanosecond, waiting for an answer back from all those points saying that everything is A-OK. If there is not an answer, the brain sends some more signals with greater intensity to "double check" why there was no response the first time. If there still is not a response the brain sends a different kind of signal looking for something, like heat, cuts, crushing, pressure or contractions. If return signals are still not received, then the brain hunts for an explanation. It tries to match the movements of the other side of the body, or fulfill what the eyes have seen from a lifetime of experiences. The brain is like a toddler, constantly asking "why", continually trying to get an answer. If the nerves will not tell the truth, then the brain searches my imagination to fill in a story, from science class, from my life, from a horror movie, or from my childhood monsters. The brain is a control freak, and will not stop searching or creating until it has its answer. A good example of this phenomenon is banging my invisible elbow, when I go around a corner too sharply or get physically too close to something. My eyes and brain have known for almost 50 years that I am 5'9" and my shoulders are about this wide, my arms are this long and if I get so close, I will bang into something, and then it should hurt. Guess my brain hasn't gotten the memo yet, about the surgery and that I am now running a little short handed on that side. Time may change the intensity, but right now, it just exhausts me.

The additional 600 mg's of Neurontin were finally

easing the flames and the tearing flesh. I stretched out on the couch, making sure the blanket did not rub against my cheek, which could start a completely new set of flaming sensations. If I could just sleep for a few hours, just rest for a little bit, just get away from my arm for a few moments, just dream about skydiving. The tall antique clock chimed four, and I could feel a strong breeze, which was confirmed by the bright orange windsock looking like a giant cartoon carrot. The Colorado blue skies are boldly vivid and blue. The faint white wispy clouds seem to waltz across the endless high altitude horizon. The drought and summer heat have turned all the prairie grasses a light dusty brown, so the ribbons of black interstate and straight airstrip stand out boldly in contrast. The noise of the small plane drones out any conversation and all I can hear is my own heartbeat against my helmet. I check my camera, leg straps, scan the horizon, check our location compared to the drop zone, and look at the altimeter on my wrist, which reads 04:56. My heart races, that altitude is too low, then I realize I am still on the couch. The darkness of night falls once again and the house is quiet. My hands

83

are tingly from sleeping all bunched up on the lumpy couch. I grab my sleeve to pull up and get untangled from the wadded up blankets and "POP!" a mannequin arm pulls out of my pajamas with ketchup squirting everywhere. I look at my altimeter again and it reads 05:14. I leap to my feet and I am standing in the center of the living room, with our dog staring at me as if I'm a loony stranger. When I finally sit down on the couch, she pounces on me, licking my face and wagging her tail off. I'm glad some things never change. The warmth of her body feels good against the chilly room. Her excited heart is beating as fast as mine is, then the rhythm of our hearts pound together and soon slow down to a normal rate as we lie there in the darkness. The altimeter now reads 05:26 and the drone of the engine is so dim and far away. The cabin of the plane is so hot and bright in the morning sunshine that I can feel the sun rays bouncing off my face, and the bright light makes me turn away. I reach into my pocket for my sunglasses, but they must be in my other shirt, not these pajamas. It takes a few moments of sitting on the couch to really clear my mind, sort out what is dream, and what is reality. I am not sure if it is the

84

medication, being exhausted all the time, or this new independence my brain has found. Some days I wish it was all gone, just quiet, just nothing, just peaceful. The green numbers on the stereo say 06:03, guess its time to really get up and start the day.

I like the early part of the day the best, because some days there is no pain. Showering is uneventful, maybe because my eyes are closed and the noise of the water has sounded the same for my whole life. As my mind wakes up, a little green sprout starts working out of the stump, just like Jack & the Bean Stalk. The tiny sprouts turn into fingers and my phantom arm quickly grows into place. The invisible arm grows out and hugs down along my ribs, bent at the elbow against my belly, with my left hand held flat against my right hip in a perfect salute. It feels extra warm where my imaginary arm presses against my skin. I hesitate before shaving, because it can trigger the phantom tone for the rest of my day, depending upon which nerves are awakened in the morning. My brain continues to search for the millions of nerves that should be connected to my arm. In the quest for answers, my brain has begun to assign response signals or "feelings" to

85

other parts on the left side of my body to make up for the missing inputs from my missing arm. My left cheek is now the bottom side of my forearm, so if I am winking at you, it is probably just my arm itching. My ear has taken over where the backside of my left arm was. If I hear a sharp loud noise, or a dog barking, it sends shards of pain ripping through the imaginary muscles. The tip of my ear is now my elbow. If I bump it or lay against my ear, there is a feeling of someone hitting that sensitive elbow crazy bone with a hammer. The strokes of the razor pulling against my whisker stubble, resonates on the top of my forearm as a knife or screwdriver gouging down to the bone and then scraping the length of my arm bone, in order to match that same scratching sound as my whiskers. I still cannot decide if it is better to go very fast or let my arm calm down between shaving strokes. Some days my arm forgets to stop shaving and gouges down to the bone until it finds something better to do. This simple act of shaving may push me to growing a beard, except that each time my beard grows back now; it comes back in the most horrible shade of white. Must be from the medicines I am taking.

The mechanics of getting dressed takes longer than before the accident, and I have even mastered tying my own shoes. Driving the automatic SUV is easier than the old standard truck, but good teeth, a strong knee and some gymnastic moves makes things possible. Once at work, the high energy of my office and my fantastic customers makes the mornings go by quickly. The best trick I have found is keeping my mind focused on other things, so it does not have time to play with the invisible arm. Sometimes when answering emails or working at my computer, my arm quits hugging me or gouging the bone, and decides to crawl into the rubber bands. It starts out with a flat-handed salute, and slowly tightens the thumb and pinky finger together, then tightens the straight pointed fingers together like the head of a snake. If I fight against the tightening rubber bands to pry my fingers apart, the force to keep them together gets stronger and more violent. Sometimes even yawning and stretching with my right arm brings on the rubber bands with tremendous force and surprise. My arm seems to fight off the rubber bands on its own, by unwrapping from my waist and contracting up above my shoulder like a Ninja warrior. My imaginary left elbow pulls up and behind me until my left shoulder blade is forced into the back of my neck. Sitting in a chair is about impossible at this point, because that invisible elbow jutting out backwards pushes my balance forward, and that is when I must stand up or work from a stool. My left hand must remember my drill Sergeant from the Air Force. When my elbow goes back into the push-up stance, my wrist bends at a sharp ninety degree angle, the fingers flare for perfect balance, my bicep is flexed and taught, just waiting for the next command that Sarge will bellow out to all the grunts in olive drab, all holding that perfect planked push-up position. The count from Sarge never comes, so the invisible muscles stay tensed, and then begin to quiver under the extended pressure, shaking uncontrollably as my mind and heart start pumping to keep up with the endurance. From the exterior viewpoint, that pink stump just hangs there sleeping, oblivious to all the work and activity happening in my left arm. I try not to think about the left side activities, because that only gives my arm center stage, and gives it the power of my conscious mind also. The Neurontin and sodium blockers seem to help dim the pain, whereas muscles relaxers, Percocet, and painkillers do nothing for the pain, since the nerves are not getting responses from the imaginary or relaxed muscles.

On a rare day, the graphic pain will not be so prevalent, but my arm is always busy. On some days, it will hold a pen or carry a screwdriver, even though I am right handed. For a few days, my left hand was holding a keypad calculator, the exact same one that I carried when I was a frozen food delivery driver. My hand was so very careful to hold the keypad so it was within easy reach of my right hand and the screen was tipped so I could read it easily. I could even push the buttons with my right hand of that imaginary inanimate object, and see the numbers on the display screen change. I had to quit using the invisible calculator because people were looking at me as if I was "Rain Man". It was somewhat cool, unless I'm crazy.

Most days are a combination of sensations, pain and graphic surprises. As the day progresses, the pains quickly intensify. By mid-afternoon, my lumbering giant is back, grabbing the flesh on the bottom of my wrist and peeling it backwards to my elbow or armpit, and just letting it hang there from the bone. When the first pull tears the flesh from the bone, I have to reach over with my right hand to make sure my shirt is not wet and full of blood. After a few seconds, the dangling muscles and skin all smooth forward, as if nothing had happened. Another few seconds pass, then it starts all over again, pulling the flesh off the bone, and then smoothing it back. During this time, my left eye squints and pulls down towards the corner of my mouth. When the duration or intensity is almost unbearable, the left corner of my mouth begins to pull towards the jaw line. The lack of facial control is similar to a stroke victim, Parkinsons or a super overdose at the dentist office. I can envision a comedian's funny routine when he slacks one side of his face, complains his lips are sliding off of his face and then says with the best slurred drool, "I dwibe a webah tcheby, you knowb, a webah tcheby" as he imitates driving around a corner with an imaginary steering wheel in his imaginary red Chevy. On days like this, my mind battles with my body while I try to concentrate on the everyday tasks in front of me.

As the end of my work day finishes, the push-ups, the

calculator, rubber bands and the giant all struggle with each other to see which contortion will take control. I hope that the calculator wins, because if nothing is happening in my arm, the giant fingernail pliers take over the scene. A large pair of pliers grab the tips of my fingernails, then pulls up and backwards, pulling a tendon through the top side of my arm all the way up to the top curve of my shoulder, as if pulling the zip-string on an EZ open plastic bag. The other four fingernails are pulled out in the same manner until all five tendons dangle from the top of my shoulder. Just like watching a movie in reverse, they all suck back into the cuts on the top of my arm and mend all back into place. Once I realize that I have not wet my pants, it starts all over again, and continues until the next dose of drugs take effect or until God takes it from me. Keeping highly intent or focused on other activities takes away the intense energy from the phantom pains, but when I am tired, my mind is much harder to keep distracted.

About four weeks after coming home from the hospital was the worst day that I can remember. We were still trying to find the proper medications and the proper dosages. The pliers were pulling out tendons most of the day. I could not eat, the look and smell of my phantom arm made me nauseous. My physical stump had healed well, though still a little red and puffy. My Neurontin was capped at 600mg per day, since the average patient who has some kind of back surgery only requires 200mg per day. The doctors would eventually increase my Neurontin to 3600 mg/day, so I could function in the normal world, but the pain is still never gone. On that fateful day, I was exceptionally tired. I had not slept well since surgery, and was struggling at work with my common hand tools. It was hard catching up from the few days I lost for surgery, taking so much longer to do the simplest things. My family was still grieving their loss of a normal life, and I was aching inside from not being up in the air with my friends from the drop zone. I was huddled up on the couch in total darkness, holding pressure on my head to make the thoughts and pain go away. I felt like an abandoned child, rocking, crying, trying to make sense of what the next step should be, and wondering how long I could survive like this.

Back in the air skydiving at Fremont County Airport,
Colorado.

BACK ON THE HORSE –
BACK IN THE AIR

From the first moments in the hospital after the accident, during the diagnostic phase, after the amputation, and to this day, I dream of being back up in the air skydiving. My first time back in the air was only six weeks after the accident. I decided to do a tandem jump since I was still pretty weak physically and not yet completely healed from the accident. I had broken ribs, three broken bones in my foot, broken left clavicle, scapula, and coracoid process. Matt made good on his promise in the hospital and took me up for a tandem jump. It was fantastic to be back in the sky!

My second time in the air was my first solo jump. It was just eight weeks after the accident, which took the use of my left arm, but before the amputation. To keep my limp left arm from flopping and throwing me off balance, we wrapped it in gauze and duct taped it to my torso. After 343 personal jumps, being an instructor, and working as a jumpmaster, I was now connected to a static line like a first time student. Not knowing how my balance and reactions would be, the drop zone manager wanted to make sure the static line attached to the plane would open my canopy. For years I had pulled the ripcord on my sport canopy with my left hand, because I had dislocated my right shoulder and did not have the flexibility to reach my ripcord. Now that I only had the right side, I would have to switch back to right-handed. The pilot yelled "DOOR!" and we popped the door. It felt good to feel the wind rushing in the door, buffeting under the wing again. I started to step out onto the step and grab the strut of the wing, but I could not reach all the way across my body with my right hand. My jump buddy, Nick, kept tapping me, trying to get me to move faster, as if I was a first time student. I looked back at him and he flashed that huge smile with the thumbs up signal. I wanted to tell him I lost my arm, not my mind.

He must have read my thoughts because he laughed at me and shook his head. We were getting farther from the airport so I could not wait any longer. I bailed out of the plane headfirst, just like the old days. The static line automatically pulled open my gigantic 300 square foot canopy. After years of jumping with a smaller high performance canopy of only 150 square feet, this one looked like a football field flying above me. I was able to unstow the right steering toggles but the left toggle kept blowing out of my reach. I did a controllability check with a right turn, left turn, but then could not grab both toggles in one hand for a flare, the braking maneuver to slow down a descent. I kept fumbling with the toggles, losing altitude, losing relationship to the airport, and losing all the strength in my right arm. I finally got both the toggles in one hand again, but could only half flare, because the vertical cords that connected me to the canopy were blocking my range of motion. I let go of the toggles and tried reaching around the vertical risers, but then I could not reach the left toggle. I checked my altimeter on my hand, looking for the landing area, and knew I was running out of time. I tried reaching the toggles again from the front of the risers and got enough pull to turn and face into the wind. I was lined up pretty well with the landing pit, but I still felt out of balance with my useless left arm gauzed and taped to my torso. The wind started working with me, and I flew over the tarmac, knowing that it would really hurt if I had to land there. The wind pushed me a little further so I was within 200 feet of the landing pit. I could see the windsock and was headed the right direction, directly into the wind. The ground was coming up fast and I knew I could only right turn or half flare/brake. I didn't want to spin into a hard right turn and crash into the ground so I half-flared, let go of the toggles, and got ready to land with a five point rolling fall or PLF. My two spotters on the ground were too far away, but were headed towards me if I needed help. A square landing with a dusty roll and I was safe on the ground. It took a couple seconds to get up, and then I collapsed my canopy so the wind would not catch it and drag me through the dirt. My spotters could see that I was up and all right. My first thought was – mission accomplished –1ArmSkydiver back in the air! My second thought was the relief that I did not hit the tarmac, did not land in the cactus, and did not break my helmet camera. I felt good to be living again.

My second solo jump was both better and worse than the first jump. The best part was that I would free fall, instead of being on a static line. My right arm and shoulder had been doing everything for me for the last ten weeks, so I was surprised how mobile and flexible my "bad" shoulder had become. This right shoulder now did all the dressing, clothing, shaving, carrying, feeding, working, typing and driving – all solo. I was able to pull my ripcord with no problem, but I still fought to keep control of the steering toggles, and ended up steering with the rear risers. I got much closer to the landing pit this jump, but still came in with the rolling PLF landing. The worst part about this jump was that I forgot to turn on my helmet camera! Chad was on the ground watching me, and was excited that it looked like a textbook PLF landing. It was great to have a good landing, but now my goal was to have a standup landing.

With all my medical needs and trying to get set up for my amputation, I was only able to skydive every other weekend. I started using a large carabiner to join my steering toggles together, so I could more quickly change my steering from the back or the front. I was still getting too tired to make more than a couple jumps in one day. On my fifth and sixth solo jumps, I finally had a stand up landing. I was using my new Racer Firebolt 218 canopy. I had purchased this custom built canopy from another one-armed skydiver who had it custom made for him. Our drop zone has grown and has gotten more trained instructors and jumpmasters, so there is more time for fun jumps. I now have the time to focus on my jumps a little more but I sorely miss the excitement and enthusiasm of my students.

The most nerve wracking thing about only having one hand while skydiving is having enough time after exiting the aircraft, and following a student on a static line. Leaving the plane at only 3,500 feet, getting stable, pulling the pilot chute, joining the steering toggles together with a carabiner, and then flying to the landing pit does not allow much time for errors. The second most difficult thing, is switching from pulling the steering toggles from behind the risers or in front of the risers. When pulling with my hand facing forwards, the steering

100

is normal, but after reaching around to the front, with my hand facing back towards me, the rights and lefts are reversed. It is in the last few moments of descent that I must switch to the front of the risers so I can flare or brake my canopy. That is when decisions and steering are the most critical and that is when things get backwards. I think that steering is the hardest thing to "learn" since the old way was so engrained in my mind. This will probably be the hardest thing to teach someone else. It will be something they have to feel when it works right.

Being up in the air is an emotional thrill and a physical test of what my body can do. Jumping configurations with other seasoned divers is exciting during the creative planning stage and fulfilling when the plan actually works up in the air. Sometimes it takes a couple tries to get the plan to work but the teamwork and beating a challenge make those jumps even more intense. Many people ask why I like skydiving so much and why I would risk going back up into the air again. I think the biggest reason is jumping with students. Seeing the raw emotions in their faces helps me judge how ready they truly are. Some are full of excitement, hesitation, concern, laughter, fear, unknowing, and sometimes a combination of all of these. Getting to hear their first words and thoughts when they are back on the ground is always a thrill and sometimes very surprising. Their smiles and excitement fill the air with so much energy that you can almost touch it. I like being able to teach someone something they wouldn't normally do, to push their comfort zone, and help them achieve a goal they have put in front of themselves. I like seeing people succeed at their dreams.

The climb to the top of Mt. Elbert, Colorado with the No Barrier's Group.

WHAT BARRIERS?

On June 3, 2012, I climbed Mount Elbert in Leadville, CO. This peak is 14,433 feet to the summit, and is one of the great "Fourteeners" in the state. I was invited to go with the group "No Barriers" led by Erik Weihenmayer. He is the only blind person to climb the tallest peak on every continent including Mount Everest. His group fundraises and supports individuals to get outdoors and embrace the No Barriers mindset and discover "what's within you is stronger than what's in your way." The No Barriers programs are designed to immerse participants, leaving them believing in the power of the human spirit to transcend all barriers. They have many programs including "Soldiers to the Summit", "Global Explorers" and their annual No Barrier Summit held in various locations around the world.

The night before the 2012 No Barriers Summit climb, a kick off dinner was served and we were able to mingle and meet other climbers. Some were blind, some were amputees, some were veterans, some needed climbing companions, some were adaptive, and some were there as supporters. The thread that brought all of us together is that we are willing to try to beat a barrier. The theme of the event was "What is YOUR Everest?", focusing on things from everyday tasks to major life challenges.

Sandy and I were fortunate to sit at the table with Erik Weihenmayer. I have watched so many of his videos and visited his website at www.nobarriersusa.org to learn about all the things he does. He recently took up the sport of kayaking. He uses other kayakers around him to yell directions and become his eyes. His reaction time is instantaneous and his trust in his guides is astounding. I am amazed at all he can do without vision, which I think would be so difficult.

After finishing the salad course of the dinner we were served a plate of pasta, which included a large basil leaf. Erik picked up that basil and exclaimed, "Someone put a leaf in my pasta!" We all busted up with laughter, feeling more at ease with this famous person. Erik is super personable and fun to be around. I was glad to get to ask him why he chose kayaking, what the things he enjoyed the most were, and the technical side of how he does certain things. After speaking a while, he then asked me how I kept from tumbling or barrel rolling when skydiving since I was lopsided and out of balance. That was an easy question; I just use my right arm in front of me like a rudder on a boat. He laughed, and shared how we have adapted to doing things that many people take for granted and may not even appreciate. The high altitude thin air and the wonderful dinner made us unusually sleepy. We headed for our room in order to be rested for the next day's climb.

The next morning was a beautiful Colorado morning, crisp air, clear skies and snow flecked mountains surrounding us. I have been active since my accident and amputation but nothing strenuous like weight training or cardio workouts. I would walk for a while and then rest if the people in front of me stopped. Some people would hustle on by and some would stop to talk and meet everyone they ran into. I hiked much of the trip with a blind climber and his lead man. They had a bell attached to one of the guide's trekking poles so he could hear the pathway. If there was a log or boulder in the pathway, the guide would call out what kind of obstacle it was, and the best way to go over or around it. It was interesting to watch their teamwork. At timberline, I was about ready to call it quits, however the blind team was still going so I kept moving along with them. There is a false summit about 500 feet from the top which was a little disappointing but made the last push well worth the extra effort. We took pictures and flew the No Barriers flag. It was worth the five hours to climb to the top and another three hours of descent. My old knees were feeling the burn much more on the down trip than the climb up. This will be one of the days I will remember the rest of my life; people working together to make the difficult dreams possible.

AEP – Amputees Empowering Partners, is an interactive website that has become a great way to meet other amputees and get new ideas on how to overcome obstacles. It has opened the door to meet young and old all across the country. Being able to see others, and how they have adapted, the tools they use, the specialty clothing that makes things more comfortable, and hearing some of their personal stories is such an encouragement to me. Just becoming aware of the large numbers of amputees from auto accidents, cancer and blood clots astonished me. There seems to be a wide range of attitudes from the survivors depending upon their age. The older people seem to have more trouble with the speed of the physical recovery but are much more at peace with their situation because they have already experienced most of their life. Perhaps the younger set is just more comfortable sharing their feelings. They seem quicker to heal physically yet more disturbed that the rest of their life will be altered. Some of the very young do not even seem to know they have a struggle ahead of them; it is just the way their life has always been. The thing I like the best with this website is that it breaks down the walls of being able to talk openly and not offend anyone with honest and sincere questions or thoughts. I was raised in a small town during a time when it was rude to look at someone with a disability. It was forbidden to talk to "them".

Those souls with physical disabilities were sent away and did not get to stay with the love and support of their families. Educating people and having an open forum is changing how we treat each other.

September 1 is opening day of the dove hunting season in Texas. I was invited by Ashley Kurpiel to attend the One Arm Dove Hunt in Texas. The event is organized to bring arm amputees together. I will be attending with my father, who taught me to hunt in Texas so many years ago. My pump shotgun was too clumsy and dangerous for me to load, pump and shoot with only one hand. I found a pistol grip, semi-automatic shotgun that will help me control my shots and I will not have to load between every shot. The barrel is a longer hunting barrel, as compared to most of the tactical pistol grip shotguns. Without a second hand to support the weight of the barrel, my right arm will be getting a super duty workout. I am excited to meet other shooters to see how they have overcome their special needs.

Dress up for the Zombie Walk in Pueblo, Colorado.

OUTTAKES

Similar to the outtakes at the end of movies, funny things arise because of the loss of my arm. It is not out of disrespect or callousness, but life happens in the oddest ways when we are busy trying to live.

"The Elbow Hold"

As simple as this may sound, I've tucked a clipboard, notebook or newspaper under my arm for many years. To this day, when I am in a hurry, my right hand does the quick handoff and the item falls quickly to the floor. Most times I pretend that it merely slipped out of my right hand unless I start laughing, then it is a dead

113

giveaway.

"Costumes"

Making people laugh has been on my agenda since grade school, and the school principals across Texas can attest to it. This summer I attended the "Zombie Walk at the Riverwalk" in Pueblo. It was not a corporate event, but a Facebook explosion. Hundreds of people showed up in their best Zombie wear and had their slow-paced parade. Lots of red lipstick, dark eye-liner, an old ripped T-shirt, my fake plastic arm, and I was ready for the party. Being weird and gross was part of fitting into this crowd. Some people would give the quizzical look trying to figure out my 'costume'. Some would come up and want to have a feel, and some even wanted to take pictures with me. The best part of activities like this is that I can cross the barrier of fear and curiosity. It is easier for people to talk, to learn, to understand and to see beyond the disability when in a more casual atmosphere. I can hardly wait for Halloween!

"Swimming"

For Father's Day, my wife and kids all took me to the river for tubing, swimming and playing in the water. Wet slick inner tubes squirt out from underneath you with little provocation, and getting back upon them is half the fun. We scrambled with each other to be king of the tube or execute stealth submarine attacks to flip over an unsuspecting rafter. My teenagers were all full of energy and roughhousing that day, tipping and dunking each other. My balance for diving was now different, but a couple practice jumps brought back childhood energy and confidence. After several hours, the currents of the river started overcoming my lopsided strength. My last dive of the day took me to the bottom of the swimming hole, but with only one arm, I couldn't pull myself to the surface. I kicked with all my heart, but merely curved under the water, I couldn't pierce the surface. What seemed like hours, was probably only twenty to thirty seconds; a fight I thought I was losing. I only had the strength for one last kick. The ironic thought of falling 3,000 feet out of the sky and surviving, yet drowning in eight feet of water exploded in my head. Perhaps it was an adrenaline rush or God's grace, but all of a sudden I could see the bright Colorado sunshine and finally fill my empty lungs with precious air. My kids parked me on a rock and worried about my condition. I was exhausted, cold and shaky. My body has trained, run, survived and fought under the harshest conditions. This total weakness was new to me and it was a stark reality check that my physical abilities have changed.

"Would you cut my steak?"

I was at a wedding reception with friends, and the meal was a delicious steak dinner. After our table had been served, I asked our server if she would take my steak back to the kitchen and have them cut up my steak. She hesitated and thought for a moment. As she slowly reached for my silverware, she explained that the knives in the kitchen were no better than the knife I had sitting on the table. I broke into a broad smile, to help ease her doubts. I leaned towards her and explained softly that the knife was adequate, but I only had one hand to operate it, and holding a fork in my mouth looked really tacky at a special event like this. She stood upright and looked at me in disbelief, then broke into a grand smile as she realized that I was not joking with her. All of a sudden she made eye contact, and finally saw me. Her quick steps had my steak dinner back to me, in perfect style. The other guests at the table would have gladly helped me, but I rather let them enjoy their meals. A few minutes later, the banquet coordinator came to our table and asked if there was a problem with my meal. I explained how our server had taken care of me, and that it was my arm, not their food. This simple task has improved my dining experiences at all restaurants. When ordering my steak dinners, I now request that the chef cuts up my steak. My dinner is easy to pick up and the chef can peek inside to confirm that his grilling is to perfection.

"Meet and Greet"

After my accident I was determined to get back to skydiving, but my physical limitations could cause dangerous situations. I did research on amputee skydivers and the equipment that is available. Having only one arm, it could get dangerous using a typical two handle emergency system. Reaching for the red cut-away handle then reaching across my body for the second silver emergency ripcord handle, and getting them both pulled in a matter of seconds might not work properly if I ever experience a failure. I posted an ad on www.dropzone.com to purchase a canopy and rig with an S.O.S. System. A Single Operation System provides one handle that allows for half a pull to break away from a faulty canopy and the remainder half of the pull to deploy the emergency chute. I received numerous replies from others wanting to sell their old student SOS rigs. I received one reply from another one-armed skydiver, Mike Boland. He warned me about buying worn out junk that would not fit my needs. He had an SOS rig that was designed for him by Racer, a company that manufactures specialty canopies for non-standard divers. They make canopies for extra small, extra tall, special speeds, high performance acrobatics, and special physical needs. This canopy has a flatter top and extra lines on the rear for easier braking, since we both only have one arm to pull against the wind. Mike said he would be glad to sell me this rig for a bargain, since he had quit skydiving. We talked and set up a time to meet. Being a mechanic for an airline, he hopped on a plane after work, brought me the canopy and flew back in time for his next shift. He always gets odd looks when he brings his own parachute through security and onto the plane. As we discussed locations, I asked how I would recognize him. There was a long pause on the other end of the line and a calm voice spoke to me, "Guess I'll look pretty much like you, one arm and a parachute!" We laughed on the phone and again when we met in the airport. It was encouraging that he was happy and at peace with his own situation and was willing to help me get back in the air. He joked and teased me that we were both "all right" since we both are missing our left arms. What an inspiration and example of peacefulness.

Street festivals and events at our local Riverwalk are great entertainment throughout the summer. Having the Professional Bull Riders here brings all sorts of rodeo and western talent to summer celebrations. Sandy, the kids, and I were watching one of the trick ropers entertain the crowds. We were seated in the front row on a bail of hay, while Sandy flmed his amazing performance for YouTube. During part of the show the roper used his bullwhip to snap a bottle cap off the top of his head. The winds were high that day and he was having difficulties just keeping the target from blowing off his head. The crowd had gotten involved and were laughing and heckling him, to which he always had a spontaneous and witty comeback. He joked and danced around the stage explaining how dangerous this was and he could lose his head if he wasn't careful. Of course I had to stand up and say, "That's exactly how I lost my arm!" as I put my hand and stump up into the air. The crowd roared and the roper was caught speechless for the first time. As we were getting up to leave after the show, the roper came up to us and stuck out his hand to greet me. He laughed and gave me grief about stealing the show, but was glad that I was a good sport. We talked about his talent and my accident. We joked about the possibilities of new comedy that a one armed bandit could bring to his show. It's amazing where a friendship can start, just by investing a little time and laughter.

"Kids Say the Darnedest Things"

"Out of the mouths of babes"… is so true. Some of the best questions about my amputation have been from young children. They ask questions from their heart with honesty and curiosity. Some parents pull their children away or discourage them from speaking to me. One little girl about four years old asked where my hand was. I explained that it had been hurt and the doctors had to cut it off. She would not accept a simple answer until she looked up my sleeve, and could see that I was not hiding it under my shirt. I thought it was very astute that she wanted to know what the hospital did with my arm. I wanted to know also.

"Special Delivery"

Being back to work with my customers, suppliers and co-workers helped me heal and get back to "normal". There becomes a familiar routine with the many people that I help and the various customer service people that help my business run smoothly. Our postal carrier had our route for years and one day we had a new guy. I was sitting at the workbench when he came in, dropped the mail and took our out going envelopes. I noticed immediately that he had a prosthetic leg, so I wanted to talk to him to see if he had any phantom pain. I hollered at him from the work area, "Hey one-legged man I'm a one-armed man and I want to talk to you." He turned quietly and left the room to deliver mail to the dentist office upstairs. I ran out into the foyer and again hollered after him, "Hey one-legged man, I'm a one-armed man and I want to talk to you." He left the dentist office and headed out the front door. Now I felt bad, that I may have offended him by being so bold, so I ran to the truck to apologize and set things straight. He slid the door shut in my face and looked to the far side of the truck, sorting his next set of deliveries. I'm not usually at a loss for words, but I was shocked at his actions. I slapped the door of the truck and said, "Hey!" The poor guy almost jumped out of his skin he was so surprised by the noise. He looked at me and held his left hand to his ear and spoke in a monotone voice, "I no hear, I no hear." He could read lips very well and we talked about what happened to him. He had fallen in a mountain climbing accident, shattering his leg beyond hope of any repairs. He did not have much phantom pain, but his prosthetic leg was hot and sweaty in the summer, and would cause heat rash on his stump. We see each other around town, and always make a few minutes to catch up on what has been happening in our lives.

WHAT NEXT??

In the time since my accident and amputation, the world has been going ten thousand miles an hour. My priorities have changed and my appreciation for those around me has increased. I've always thought that helping others was part of why we are put together on this planet and now it has become a part of my everyday life. I want people to see that even though my physical body is different, I still enjoy my life tremendously and am excited about how many people might be encouraged by my story. My strength comes from a strict upbringing and years of taking care of myself. Responsibility, faith and hard work prepped me for the greatest opportunity of my life. Knowing God got me through all of the last fifty years making it easier to know that the next years will be equally blessed, yet they will be phenomenally different. My hope is that others pick up the torch of kindness and support and get involved, just as so many people have jumped in to help me. Some days I start to wonder what I would be doing today if my life had remained "normal". I am where I am and I have two choices: to move forward from here or give up. It sounds too simple to just keep on trying, yet some days that is the only thread of energy that I have.

So many people have been supportive and encouraging that I am amazed how intertwined our lives and connections have become. It is astonishing to know this is just the beginning of my next chapter in life. My medications and physical limits may affect my health in the next decade, but until then I want to clasp onto the people and adventures that are filling my life. Hopefully our paths will cross, but until then...

BLUE SKIES!!

1ArmSkydiver

RESOURCES & OTHER STORIES

www.1armskydiver.com
www.clasplife.com
www.highskyadventurespc.com
www.dropzone.com
www.geocaching.com
www.nobarriers.com
www.AEP.com

MSNBC-TV Caught on Camera
"Up in the Air"

Pueblo Chieftain
"A Gift to Remember" 12/30/2011

Travel Channel:
"When Vacations Attack" Episode #205

Pueblo Chieftain
"Mighty Force of Human Spirit" 6/18/2012

FOLLOW TOMMY FERGERSON

Website:

http://www.1armskydiver.com

Twitter:

https://twitter.com/1armskydiver

Facebook:

https://www.facebook.com/tommy.fergerson

YouTube:

http://www.youtube.com/user/1armskydiver

LinkedIn:
http://www.linkedin.com/pub/tommy-
fergerson/55/348/159